INTO EACH ROOM
WE ENTER WITHOUT KNOWING

Crab Orchard Series in Poetry
First Book Award

INTO EACH ROOM
WE ENTER WITHOUT KNOWING

POEMS BY CHARIF SHANAHAN

Crab Orchard Review &
Southern Illinois University Press
Carbondale

Southern Illinois University Press
www.siupress.com

Copyright © 2017 by Charif Shanahan
All rights reserved
Printed in the United States of America

20 19 18 17   5 4 3 2

The Crab Orchard Series in Poetry is a joint publishing venture of Southern
Illinois University Press and *Crab Orchard Review*. This series has been made
possible by the generous support of the Office of the President of Southern
Illinois University and the Office of the Vice Chancellor for Academic Affairs
and Provost at Southern Illinois University Carbondale.

Editor of the Crab Orchard Series in Poetry: Jon Tribble
Judge for the 2015 First Book Award: Allison Joseph

Cover illustration: *Running Children, Morocco, 1951*, by Irving Penn, *Vogue*
(December 1, 1953), 84; © Condé Nast

Library of Congress Cataloging-in-Publication Data
Names: Shanahan, Charif, 1983– author.
Title: Into each room we enter without knowing / poems by Charif Shanahan.
Description: Carbondale : Crab Orchard Review & Southern Illinois
University Press, 2017. | Series: Crab Orchard Series in Poetry
Identifiers: LCCN 2016035391 | ISBN 9780809335770 (paperback) |
ISBN 9780809335787 (e-book)
Subjects: LCSH: Identity (Psychology)—Poetry. | Racially mixed people—
Poetry. | Arab Americans—Race identity—Poetry. | Blacks—Race identity—
Poetry. | African Americans—Race identity—Poetry. | Gays—Identity—
Poetry. | BISAC: POETRY / General.
Classification: LCC PS3619.H35442 .A6 2017 | DDC 811/.6—dc23
LC record available at https://lccn.loc.gov/2016035391

Printed on recycled paper. ♻

This paper meets the requirements of ANSI/NISO Z39.48-1992 (Permanence
of Paper) ∞

For my parents

. . . we are like siblings,
you & I, separated
by many years, & rooms.
   —Aracelis Girmay

CONTENTS

I

II

I

GNAWA BOY, MARRAKESH, 1968

The maker has marked another boy to die:
His thin body between two sheets,
Black legs jutting out onto the stone floor,
The tips of his toenails translucent as an eye.
Gray clumps of skin, powder-light,
Like dust on the curve of his unwashed heel
And the face, swollen, expanding like a lung.
At its center, the sheet lifts and curves:
His body's strangeness, even there.
One palm faces down to show the black
Surface of hand, the other facing up
White as his desert's sky.
                                        As if underwater,
He passes from that room into the blue
Porcelain silence of the hall, where the light-
Skinned women have gathered in waiting:
No song of final parting, no wailing
Ripped holy from their throats:
The women do not walk into the sun,
They hide their bodies from it
(those pale wrists, those pale temples):
They do not walk the streets,
They do not clutch their own bodies,
They do not hit themselves in grief—

Another time, on their bed, he called out
holding a .38 against her neck
slurring something about freedom. And she

repeating the Arabic name she'd given him—
Salim: the kind, the undamaged—
paled like flame, an empty cocoon,

separating, dispersing.

From the hallway, I watched him step down
and walk out of the room, running
his hand through my hair as he crossed

the threshold. Composed, turning
to glance at the clock, she closed her robe
and asked me to take the chicken from the freezer.

PLANTATION

When he finally brought the hammer down
One half inch from my mother's face

The hole in the wall
Wide as a silver dollar

I was close enough
Huddled there

In the folds of her lap
Her arms wet with sweat and crossed

Against my back
And since from the room

All sound had gone
I was clear enough to see inside

The cracked plaster:
A river delta, fractured,

Branching off and becoming
The sea . . . Or, a tiny moon

On a shore of white sand
The tide lapping it in foam and tugging—No,

Twelve dead presidents perched there
Each with the face of my father—

Tight-lipped, vacant-eyed—
Scanning the field for a body to mark

Then locking in on her knee-bent dread—
Ordinary, mammary—

A yellow suckling heavy on her tit . . . No,
I think it was her one good eye

Refusing to blink,
Scaling the bare-white wall

At the core of the mind
(not measuring its height),

Then circling a waterless well
In a desert without sand,

Unnumbered sisters
Caught in the belly of the boats—

Where there was too much sound to hear,
Though only one voice, one cry—

Their dark arms like trellised vines
Crossed and reaching.

INTO EACH ROOM WE ENTER WITHOUT KNOWING

A boy dyes his shirt the iridescent sky
of dawn—or is it dusk? Rouged and glittered

he begins, smacking his lips as he slinks
into the club's deep bass hum.
                              Older men,
on display by the bar, slip off their tees—
leading the child

a labor of word, lyre, bark—
Ecstatic, he lurks into the back room,
                              slipping his tongue
through the body's shutters.
Floorboards unhinge. A skein of teeth unravels.

What pattern of occasion will free him?

A prayer rug for a strict occasion.
A patch of sand, enclosed within a mesh fence,

where women in headscarves kneel in sajdah,
hot from the day's sun, a pleasure this agony

of warmth and muscle: knee to sand, head to sand.
A pleasure: restraint from lamb and water,

the empty carafe, the scales of fish,
meatless and hanging to dry,

the grapes never to become wine.

Eating grapes, my friend harangues me
about the state of affairs in Riyadh.

His lips are wet, he is driving a Nissan rental.
At a streetlight, a single blackstart lands

on the side-view mirror: a lore of midnight
and melancholy song. "This Arab spring,"

my friend continues, my friend stops . . .
"Yes," I say, thinking of the blackstart

somewhere in a baobab by now.

Somewhere, a mother faints at the butcher
when a lamb's tongue is cut from the head—
the butcher pressing his fingers into
the eye sockets for leverage—

                    and the vague cool
of the air passing through the room awakes her
          as when Muḥammad awoke
in the night desert: no spruce to shade the dead
meat of him, no wind, not even stars—
      a single blackstart lands on his knee:
                   and as the mother exits
another boy begins his journey to the city,
wearing yellow sandals and a ring on each finger.

MASSA CONFUSA

A body was left me.
I did not put it on:
Two densities of bone,
Two methods of eye.

In the spleen an oasis,
An oasis as mirage—
All my people burned
On either side of me.

SELF-PORTRAIT IN BLACK AND WHITE

If I said I did not want to live anymore,
Would you understand that I meant *like this*?

The years form a mythology I can almost explain.
I see in colors because they are always so much

A part of the problem:

A fire engine is a backpack and my father.
Dollar bill is headscarf, star and crescent.

Candy cane is barbershop and my choice of men.
Gray is skin, the bridge in the center of your eye—

Now, stirring milk into my coffee with a bent spoon,
I stir milk into my coffee with a bent spoon.

ON THIS HARD BENCH

you look at me, i look away
to the swan in the canal—
everything here has meaning:
my luggage, your cigarettes,
our undone shoelaces,
the water, the park.
i speak with meticulous finality,
each word its own sentence,
and you listen as to a sermon,
hoping that the moral can be
forgiveness is divine. i am ashamed
to have been so typical, i am
ashamed even to sit up straight,
to show any firmness or strength.
i tell you i have a reservation
at a hotel down the road,
i can leave tomorrow—
neither of us speaks. evening turns
a pale green neither of us sees,
two men deaf to the city bells,
the slow water, the electric
pull of trams urging us to go.
though smaller than me, you grab
my big suitcase, my shoulder
and tell me to follow you home.

Morning dark thins. I fumble to grab my briefs from the floor
when that man in me who's not me but tells me when I'm not living well
rings the alarm, declaring all suffering a luxury, unnecessary, and I,
jeans open and back bare, charge out the door and down the stairs,

as when I heard the crash that took my other life, as when that man
in me who's not me but has a voice like mine rang the schoolyard bell
like the nuns who grabbed and dragged me by the collar, when that man
inside, still voiceless, first began to grow, when the men around me began

to gleam with some kind of holy spark I wanted to swallow—

when I speak   in my own voice
my voice clamors   smacks of men
flitting on my tongue

                        the tongues
of the many men   each pointed or flat
but always cold   and yes

I have had enough   I am going
a ribbon around my ankle
a ribbon in my hair

                 my mother
once cracked open like a jar of coins
on the floor   her high school friend

found dead on the beach   drowned
(they said)   fully-clothed   and the wave
in the picture of it

                     frozen sepia
liquid   sad amniotic liquid   white frill
at the edges   the dress she wore in '77

one year after landing here   her voice
accented like a peacock's tail
like a cup of tea with aperol

I knew that he would say "I love you"
To his wife on the phone from Canada.
Stood in my underwear in the doorway
Of their bedroom, arms around my stomach,
Thinking first, "Who is he trying
To fool?" and then, "God—how must
She feel." Snapping the phone shut,
He refused eggs, and I insisted. Rested
On the cliff in the back of my mind
Observing him not question, not squirm;
Bump into walls and simply change
Direction. After eggs, I refused sex
And still hungry, he insisted. Took off
My clothes before the bed could catch
This mess. Cleanly swallowed me all.

SOHO (LONDON)

I don't tell you that
some mornings I lean
against the bedroom wall
with one hand on my chest

           that at night
when I walk through the screens
of light from street lamps,
there's a window I can see through
to myself. I'm trying
to find my way,
past painted-over murals
in alleys, past
the locked-up shops,
the gated lots.
         I don't tell you
when I pass the club teeming
with men in glitter, I am
full of lust
and pity: I want us
to put our clothes back on and go.

        I think I am close
when I pass a stranger
and think
I could love you

          even if he doesn't turn
to greet me
       as I stand on the curb
          counting the seconds
against his back.

By now, we are used to this routine—
the airports, the trains, the long,
deliberately silent farewells.
I wait until the train doors close.
The dirty glass window between us,
I turn to exit the platform. Zürich waits
for you and I ride the escalator out
of Penn Station, past the pretzel carts,
onto the smoky streets ravaged by
the absoluteness of winter. I do not know
if I love you. There is nothing for me here
in this angry, automatic city, and you
promise me love, a home, even money.
I notice no one, walking to the subway
toward another fatherless night
in the Bronx, where I'll sit in silence,
drinking hot tea to scald the place
in my body where the pain roots.

ORIGIN

That evening, while the pasta simmered,
the man said to the woman

"Let them be white . . ."
                            And as though the earth
rumbled and shook—or rather grew

from inside a slate of nothing,
three gold-skinned balls spun into the air

and broke open: many years later,
when my arms and legs turned solid and cold,

my throat a canal, my whole body a bridge,
the saltwater stilled and darkened:

the man and the woman, turning off the stove,
poured wine into goblets marked by *X*s

and slow danced, the decision made.
Now in the cloudy glass I imagine I see

empty hands filling themselves with other hands,
letters I can almost decipher—yes,

tell me I belong here, diving
into my own center: my own self

an unknowable reef—

II

How easy for the waterfall to turn back
into the river, the long, silent face
holding all that has passed through it
as though untouched,
undisturbed. . . . Then, within it,
a shadow moves—a turtle, or
kelp wavering, drifting, reaching,
trying to exist beyond its own watery nest—
and the face darkens,
quickens, stills. The waterfall
insists on its own incessant breaking, an anxiety,
a completion at once its own negation,
merging at its most opaque
with the waiting body, froth gathering, evaporating.
Sometimes I'll come this far from home
merely to taste the air,
the always witness to this relentless constructed flow
unable to hold itself
beyond the falling of its own nature,
asserting itself only to destroy
itself. The sky is
sunless, ill-fitting, unhinging, barely awake. The river,
taking its motion from the surging above, urges,
persists, knowing
no way out, no way to extract
itself from its own circular endurance,
tenacious, whole, singularly minded
until it carries itself back to its own source.

TIPPU TIP ON HIS DEATHBED IN STONE TOWN

I know my body holds
             the same dark as those I kept and sold
my beard   a net of routes we took to cross that land
                    in me from me with me
                         and what of you now
if I had left you there beside the village sea
     heavy bass slipping from your fingers
               in the shadow of our mast
what of hope   if I had failed—

Please—   I could see no other way
                    I had to believe
gun body bread cane   forgive me   sister mother land

HOMOSEXUALITY

i. New York

These days, my sympathy narrows:
in the Barracuda, I sip a dirty martini,
my back against the bar:
                          in the half-lit glitz
marionettes bloom from the ceiling,
the walls: slack and stringless
they fumble into each other
always about to fall—

ii. Casablanca

My uncles find wives at the souk.
Nabillah and Latifa were sisters,
now sisters-in-law: at home,
preparing couscous, they slip gin
into their buttermilk, their men
at the window calling down
to boys on bicycles.

iii. Laramie

iv. Florence

And are you here, too, dear Brunetto?
    If I had not in those days found you
among the other poets in the ghetto,
    would I now be here, passing through
this place, guided by the elder to the skies
    above the sky? How could I, alone, issue
these words—this music in our sighs?
    Give me your book, your exiled hands.
I will hold them, as your unreadable eyes,
    and walk with reverence on burning sands.

v. California

"This initiative measure is submitted to the people in accordance with the provisions of Article II, Section 8, of the [state] Constitution.

This initiative measure expressly amends the [state] Constitution by adding a section thereto;"

vi. Newark, NJ; Cypress, TX; Greensburg, IN; Tehachapi, CA

Facebook asks, What's on your mind?: "Jumping off the gw bridge sorry" MOOD
No note. (3x)

vii. Zürich

As though, recklessly,
we burn the old parchments in unison, cleansing
the walls with their smoke—
as though our bodies themselves have magnetized—

like at night when I enter the room to join you in bed
and you, still asleep, reach out for me.

LITTLE SAVIORS

So many men playing god.

Father left a wounded child

Cavorting in the public bathroom.

So many holes being filled.

EUNUCH

I.

behind the village wall   his wrists tied
with rope staked into sand   his voice has no body
his loincloth balled up and pressed flush
against the perineum   warm copper
hammered thin and sharp
circles him there   his smoothest flesh
if not early morning it is exactly noon
his eyes roll back into frenzied lids
    before the rip into him
                 and the great wound
covered in sweet wood ash and at last
the long sleep while dogs eat the blood-meat
discarded beside the well
      and his waking in air cooled by night
to stand squinting through low fog
at a woman being swallowed by a snake

II.

By day three, waist-deep in clay,

    he is ready, if still

        breathing, to accept

the hot needle, probing

    the lost urethra,

        his body then put back

into clay. By month six,

    the surface is a gnarl

        of skin, discolored,

a quilt of yellow moons,

    a shadow of hunger,

        as a hand removed

from earth remembers

    how it felt to be

        submerged,

to enter another warmth

    and then to be without—

You spoke like
I'd done more than just exist—
An echo of the schoolyard bell
We heard all the time, even at home
Years later, a continent away.
You spoke *Not like us.* You spoke
*Cracker, please. With skin like that
You ain't with us.* You said it like
You were the only one who knew:
Hovering over that dark,
Thick line means *Neither nor,* means
Can't sit here, means *Save the "half,"
You're just a nigger.* I said, *But give me
Back my father—but my mother is
An Arab.* You laughed, *Your mama's
Black as fuck.* I turned. I quit.
I said what you said, held it up
To the sun to glint, then swallowed
It back down. You said, *Child—
Black.* You said, *Cracker.* You said,
Child—Out. Out.

At Zagora's edge three rows of people,
One for each shade,
Form a half circle in the sand: the fewest are
The darkest, there in the center, waiting,
Gazing into each other's faces.
The sun rises behind them, casting red light
Onto the curves of their hands and feet.
Pulled back into the second row, a young girl—
The color not of earth, but the village
Mountain at dusk, low, double-peeked—
Hides inside the folds of her mother's robe.
Knowing not to call a hill a mountain
They wait for lamb and figs in tired order.

TICINO

For twelve months
I rode the train between two stolen cities—

cutting north or south through the Alpine green
to one of two borrowed flats,

the sunlit lake-tops assuring me
I'd need not return. Twelve months

and the border-call was always
the same—the same

indignation,
the same riled and accusatory tone:

What do you need here?
Che affari avete in Italia?

What brought me there was more
than I could say then

though I never needed to—
light skin, blue passport.

I could stay
even as the green faded into dust,

the hot earth near the border
burned out and dry

where that call waited for us—
What do you need here? Di che cosa ha bisogno?

If there was a stranger there
she was I

not the woman in the corner seat
who hearing the call

casually closed her book,
her slim brown fingers locked around its spine,

then looked out through dirty glass
at one country turning into the next—

the woman who did not turn her face
(which I imagine now was expressionless)

to meet the carabiniere's hard eyes, his hand
poised already on his holster—

she did not say a word
to his anger-lit but genuine inquiry—

the man now yelling into her silence:
Parla italiano? Do you speak Italian?

My eyes closed
on an island in a cage,

lids flickering each time
to somewhere new:

with the Gnawa in Jamaa el-Fna,
in Rome with the Roma girl

who returned my wallet for bread,
the men's hammam in el-Jadida,

at the Tallahassee Waffle House,
my four-shade family on display:

Parlo italiano? Sono italiana, signore—
in the local inflection, the tone

even and firm: *I am Italian, sir*
still looking out the window

the Alps close behind her.

Speaker + Girl
— Duality
— 2's → couplets

POST-TRAUMATIC STRESS DISORDER

At the table's end, I hunger—
not as the rash
of bees hungers

but as the eye
after the shock flash
still sees
the lightning.

"A MOUTHFUL OF SALT . . . / I CAME THROUGH NUMB WATERS"

for Morgan P.

I know my suffering is loud but my skin
is light as sky and I was told to let it

open doors, shake hands, slip the cover
over their eyes, so I could be. *Free*

is not a *negro doused in white*, blanched,
bleached, and sent down the path. *Free*

almost never means *alive*, so please try—
I'm asking for help. Whose fist is in my ribs

at which gate. What color is the room.
How do I move the line when it is buried

in the earth. Why do you think my face
is the face you think you see. In the earth.

In the water. Where do I keep my feet.
My hands. My tongue. My lungs. My eye.

All the photos taken those years
Show no people. Greek islands,
Vacant buildings and empty homes,
The bridge in Prague. All of it
Beautiful but veiled by distance.
In one photo the lighthouse of Akrotiri
Stands tall at midday (I know
From the shadow), but what I see
Even now is the black dog that followed me
Up the long path, begging for nothing,
Then vanished behind a crowd.
That's what it was like, those years.
I cannot recall a single face.
And when you ask me now I tell you
I was running,
Though the vision in my third eye is still
The same: the camera on the stone ledge
By the sea, a child's laughter
Echoing through the stone staircase.

LAKE ZÜRICH

When I arrived in evening you
drank coffee by the fireplace

ashless in winter: I knew

what slant of myself
would keep you.

At the abandoned boathouse

remnants of a party: you
placed your hand

where you knew I hurt;

I kicked a cup and leaned
into your weight.

SAINT-TROPEZ

The patio submits to the sun: my skin
now one shadow, now another,
a dark flounder that comes like thought:
his love does not feel like love
because I am small (not modestly,
not selflessly), because,
in the silence after love-making,
on the firmly made bed, here or there,
I must be met to feel whole.

UNBEARABLE WHITE

Undertone—
Cradling.

I did not know
I'd been running from it.

Unnamed
It was there, waiting

For me to see
And say,

Of course, you—
My "my."

—And so

For thirty years
An outline

Of a body
Traced into white sand

Stood firm, waving,
Calling others

To join,
Reappearing each time

The saltwater came
To wash.

PASSING

At a station in a no-name town,
a blue-red coleus

blooms from a cleft in the track.
Too obvious, I say, out loud

to the window, to God,
to no one, rolling my white eyes

into my thick bright head.
If I arrive,

who will greet me as brother,
as owner, who will greet me

at all, feeling from my veins
the pull of our one long pulse—

Pissing into the metal bin, my waste
streaming out onto the track,

I laugh at the mirror, an animal,
unhinging, trying

to see what they see
in whatever I am standing here—Then

the train slides into a long tunnel.
The lights flicker off

and I am back inside my mother.

III

As a very young woman, my mother drank a glass of bleach. Thinking it water, not tasting the burn, not smelling a single fume. At the hospital, after she had begun to breathe, the color returned to her face. The doctor warned, *One chemical will never exit your system. It won't ever leave you.* Though she has survived, she does not know it. Yesterday, on the phone, I said, *I'm beginning to understand that I am African.* And she said, *Now how can that be, child? How can that be?*

The dark matter
Turned its face to mine

And I could feel its breathing, the invisible
Pull between the invisible

Air and my half-lit face, hungry
And waiting. I felt it

Reaching for me, the sorrow-down slip
Of its call, its smoke tongue

Licking behind my ears, my hair
Erect with kinesis. I felt it

Settle on and around the table:
A slow turning: a cold tail. How

Can she sit there and say, *Child
I am not, we are not—*

In spite of—no, inside of
The dark fact of her body?

Speaker + Monster + Mother
— Tension
— Should only be two
• Mother & Monster? One!

AT *L'EXPRESS* FRENCH BISTRO MY WHITE FATHER KISSES
MY BLACK MOTHER THEN CALLS THE WAITER A NIGGER

I change the subject and ask
How long
He thinks he'll run.
He says, *Son, I am complete*
To the bone. I say, *You're evading my question.*

He says, *How's the job?*
Mom says, *Tell me how you feel.*
These days, I mutter, *black. Quite black. Pass the cream.*
He says, *What do you mean?*

To the waiter Mom says, *Bien cuit*
S'il vous plaît, smiling.
I say, *He doesn't speak French.*
Mom says, *On parle français au Maroc.* I say,
Yes, Mom. In Senegal, too.

SINGLE FILE

I don't mean who we are to each other; I mean
Who we are to ourselves.

The black slipped back into the body and suddenly I
Carried no weight at all, no memory

Of days drenched in white, no desire to white,
Because I was, I was

Becoming the dark thing they had never wanted me to be
And was, always,

Searching for the source of—what? what?
As though any of us could be

Absolved of the various,
Absolutely and permanently a single thing,

Calling past the nameless brown birds
Gathered on a single antenna, and returning

Back to itself, turning
Into a deeper version of the same thing,

Which means, colorless,
As black is.

EUNUCH (PRE-)

If a strange hair has grown,
he knows it is too late:

a soldier, then, if he is lucky—
that is, light enough.

Speaker + Identity

On stage the seller bends to the crowd.
To the few hands raised in back to bid he pleads
His palm face-up and lifted—*higher: her hard bones,*
Her skin smooth and clean—and to his right the girl,
Wearing a pearl in each ear, hides behind her arm
Raised and resting like a scarf along her face
Look at the eyes, the curve of jaw and chin, surely
A concubine
On request, he inserts two fingers, spread wide
To inspect the mouth, cocking her head back so
As to see inside her: as the auburn curtain of hair
Falls back, grazing her buttocks, her eyes lock onto
The scarved faces on the ceiling, her right leg, turning,
Bends at the knee as if to push her further into herself,
And her young body splits open for all to see.

ASMAR

for Safia E.

Dear S—
They told me again today that I was not Black:
Allison says *Even though you are Black* and what I know she is saying is
I can't believe I have to call you that.
A friend says *Just be glad you can walk through the world and be free.*
A friend says *You just tan well* and I want to ask what he is defending.
In Marrakesh a man fell down today and I had to remember why no one saw.
I lifted him to his feet. He smiled a two-tooth smile—plainly an Arab
To my eyes—and asked me where I was from. He welcomed me:
Obama! Obama! We have the same color—
Our mothers tell us we are not like them: *Les Africains sont là-bas!*
Our mothers defend what oppresses them.
Often I ask *But if I am American and my mother, wherever she's from, is Black,*
*Does that not make me—*Always I stop, knowing both answers.
In Rabat my mother's friend—they have not seen each other in 28 years—
Helps me find an apartment. She has a friend with an apartment I should see.
OK. The friend arrives in a BMW with a slave in the back. They speak in French.
My mother's friend, describing my mother, says, *C'était vraiment une belle noire:*
She was really a beautiful Black. In the backseat, I am quiet, but inside, I am saying:
She is still beautiful. She is not dead—

Or was she, to you, never living?
The purist says our mark is not Blackness and I say *What is it then*
Our mothers defend an idea of self that is not their own.
What is it then
In the slow transition from light to dark and what do we call it
When we are from halfway there? In our homes
We say *asmar asmar*—a chant of shame we cannot hear—
As the body changed with the earth and to contain it we must name it—
Asmar meaning *dark*,
Meaning *Black*,

Meaning *Nigger* (sand), meaning *Nigger*, meaning *Noir*,
Meaning *less Arab*, meaning *not fit for this life*, meaning *less*,
Meaning *how could you wed such a beast*,
Meaning *it is myself that I hate*, meaning *please do not*
Shame me, meaning *please continue to cleanse*, meaning
Insha'Allah I will not be on this earth to see your children,
Meaning *but your tongue is clean the only trace is in your lip and hair*
And it is subtle you fool, meaning *your sisters are not your sisters here*,
Meaning *I did all I could to free you why do you look back*.

SONG

I wait each night for a self.
I say *the mist*, I say *the strange
tumble of leaves*, I say *a motor
in the distance*, but I mean
a self and *a self* and *a self*.
A small cold wind
coils and uncoils in the corner
of every room. A vagrant.
In the dream
I gather my life in bundles
and stand at the edge of a field
of snow. It is a field I know
but have never seen. It is
nowhere and always new:
What about the lives
I might have lived?
As who? And who
will be accountable
for this regret I see
no way to avoid? A core,
or a husk, I need to learn
not how to speak, but *from where*.
Do you understand? I say
name, but I mean *a conduit
from me to me*, I mean *a net*,
I mean *an awning of stars*.

I drink beer in a Budapest dive. I am
here mourning my early 20s
before they are over, and I don't know
how to proceed. On the wall are
pictures of singers with pierced faces,
actors from America, a politician or two.
Even the bar owners smile, bleary-eyed
beneath the light fixture. Why
am I alone in thinking
I am not living the right life?
I don't know how to proceed.
I had believed that if I traveled,
I would find my way. I was
already a man when I left, I was
already where I am right now, sitting
in a bar in Budapest, the visible
American, invisible to himself,
a heavy sponge, watching the sun
turn away from the narrow street's walls
on the other side of the window,
where the old city inside this city
begins to stir into evening.

PREFACE

A blackstart bathes
in the deep shade of the lagoon,
six toes sinking into mud.

There is hope in the past.

I am calling out your name
all the time, I am calling

with both voices,
night and day.

[handwritten annotations:]
→ Bird → bath, cleansing
opposites
Is there? Does the speaker believe this?
no conclusion
always
duality
doubling
Blackstart, N. African bird

LANDSWEPT

Fruit flies drown
in a jar of honey;
I slice grapefruit,
kiwi, my thumb;
on the fire escape,
a Gambel's quail
bounces from bar
to bar, a rubber
band in its beak;
a triptych
at the Louvre
falls and shatters
into six; the mirror
in the hall
reflects nothing;
a bus pulls into the stop
and no one gets on;
on the South Side,
two men file
for adoption,
their brothers
behind the dunes;
a cityless expanse
consumes itself
beneath the sky's dome,
the wind the only
thing left that wants.

LIGAMENT

Even after she cut into my shoulder
Coldly, with a scalpel, resetting my clavicle,
Tying it down with borrowed ligament and screwing it
Into place, even after she sutured me shut,
Sewing the two banks of skin across the thin blood river,
Watching me sleep the chemical sleep
Until tender and hazy I awoke—Even after all that,
What seems the least plausible is how
She had known, walking into that white room,
To put her hand for just a second in my hand.

AQUA

Most mornings the window is a chest of
cold light, a muted sun rising
like my mother from the kitchen chair (my father
away with a lover) to put dinner away,
rising to come down the hallway, singing
to me about a country she once knew. Or the silence
of those days, standing at the bookshelf,
thinking the world unreal despite the fact of it.
There were times, I see now, when I wanted to die,
sitting and waiting on the solar system
comforter over my bed, the slowly lifting anchor—
when I wanted already to know what was next.
And now my brother says to me, *C—*
you have got to stop writing these fictions
in your head, and I think, *How strange that we are cast off*
in opposite directions from the very same shore.
I want to love him and the great,
unshifting wall just behind his smart eyes,
and the other brother, the secret agent in D.C.—
it's been years since we spoke, years
since he mouthed a small, quiet *Hey*
that last Thanksgiving. And by now my father has
waded so far into his own contraptions that
of course I have turned to the first colors
of morning, its reliable sky emptied out by night.

AS THE FORMLESS WITHIN TAKES SHAPE WE FAIL AGAIN

The target burrows further
from eyes and tongue,

unreachable as a self: each gesture,

each articulation of the mass
dark and inchoate inside the mind,

a release and the not-quite landing.

The poem, which does not want to state,
is the only success in this regard,

vaguely pointing in a direction.

The smell of stale compromise
Fills this Chelsea condominium,
And wreaks havoc on skin now aged
Gray with nicotine and furry air.
There are pictures of former lovers
On the mantel among a mother's,
Father's, brothers'—faded yellow
And dusty from too long a closet space.
Empty cat-food tins on the coffee table
Romance drunk bottles of Bordeaux.
A tired, loosely robed ghost moves
Past diplomas and framed chapters
Of an unwritten autobiography.
In the bedroom, sheets cover hard-
Wood floors and hold on to a corner
Of the mattress, bumpless and sterile.
Ashtrays have fallen from the desk
Into a plant pot near the window.
Outside two boys hold hands and squint
At street signs they cannot see past.

HARATIN GIRL, MARRAKESH, 1968

—As the room is emptied of the boy's body,
she watches through a hole carved into a wall of stone.
Quiet in the hall, the women carry the body awkwardly,
their pale hands tentative to touch it, grasping not the elbow or knee,
not the ankle or neck, but the rounded softnesses—
buttocks, side of torso—and the smallnesses—two fingers,
an ear, a tuft of rough hair—as if to carry him without touching him,
managing just enough to reach the end of the hall, where the girl
stares hard, her eyes strange and dark, then takes off running:
She does not begin the procession through the old city,
She does not pour the bathwater, or warm it, or salt it,
(the neighbors will not come, the body cannot be cleaned):
She does not know why she rushes down the side street
to the small rooms where her mother and siblings sit, rushing
past the boys, already men, who spend each hour in waiting
of a nameless thing that will not come, past the small violence
they call to her in their lack, that violence she lets burn through her,
or run through her, dirty water through a deep bed of sand,
stopping to curse at them, or to pray for them, if not now for
the burning in her lungs, her lungs weak with swelling, swelling
with a fear so deep she will soon no longer know it as fear,
running into the medina, losing her shoes in the running,
the bottom of her feet bruising, toenails chipped, or chipping,
her face swollen, until, suddenly, she begins to slow her pace,
noticing the blue porcelain tiles and the marriage song ahead,
or to the west, her one good eye blinded, the mind scabbing around it,
beginning to understand somewhere inside herself, in a place she feels
but cannot name, or speak from, that she will for the rest of her life
run, even when her body does not run, even as she walks,
or sits, or carries the olive hand of a child, or children, not yet born—

I climb the narrow stairs to my attic bedroom.
The riad next door is so close I reach my hand
through the one small window to touch it.
Spread my fingers wide against the stone,
stretching each in its own direction. Far away
I hear an old man singing a song to God.
My ego keeps me alive, not ready to give up its chance.
I walk down the stairs and wander the medina.
Sit at a café near the souk and order mint tea.
I want to enter my life like a room. Blue walls.
A floor painted green. Three large windows. Light.
I study the faces that pass. Count each one.
It is a long time before my eyes meet another's.

IV

"YOUR FOOT, YOUR ROOT"

At the famous deli on Houston Street, I sit opposite my father. *Stop causing trouble*, he says, *always asking questions about the heavy shit*, though I think I'm only trying to live. I ask him: *How do you see me?*, already knowing his answer, but needing a way in. He says, *Cosmetically you are white*, by which I know he means *I want to see myself in you.*   ↳ Bleach

But I've never felt white a day in my life, I say, biting into my pork sandwich. *And anyway, Dad, race isn't only about the body—you should know that by now.*

Correction
* ╱ Directive
   ╲ multiple attempts

On the air between us, I see my father in all denim beside his new '76 Chevy, a puff of blond hair, a wide, mostly joyful smile, his eyes showing only a hint of distance. The main part of his life is about to begin. My father is talking, both in the image and at the table, but I cannot make out his words.

The words: *Horse, donkey, mule*

The words: *There is no identity*

The words: *One plus one equals three*

I ask him to tell me what it was like, and he says, *My family wanted to make your mother beg for their love.* Our waitress smiles at me as she passes our table; she is Moroccan like my mother, though fair, fairer even than my father. She knows us. We've come here before. She and my mother became quick friends, exchanging numbers and recipes.

Because she was Black, I say, at once asking and stating.

No, he says. *Because she believes that she is not.*

*

Not with these words, but with a grimace as she studies Brandy and Monica in "The Boy Is Mine" video on MTV, my Omi explains: *In our land, the Black man is considered to be inferior—more primal, certainly more African—than the Arab, so as, at least subconsciously, to differentiate and elevate the Arab in valor or stature, though he remains inferior to the European, whose presence the Arab reveres and aspires to possess.*

The words she does offer are *hada sweena, hada khiba*, pointing at the TV screen: *That one is beautiful, that one is ugly.* They are roughly the same complexion. Brandy wears her hair in braids, Monica hers bone-straight, so I do not need to ask how she means what she means.

I am trying to tell you something important. I want you to know that it doesn't matter what you are, what Mom is, or believes herself to be, or not be. I was born here. When I suckled her breast, I drank it all down. I don't mean that figuratively.

↳ Bleach

He says, *C—do you consider the temperature in the room when you are neither hot nor cold? Do you think about food when you are not hungry?* I stare at him and say, *Really, Dad? Rhetorical questions? Riddles?* He says, *No, no—I'm telling it to you as plainly as I can.*

*

I stand up, pushing my chair away from the table with my legs. A man outside shuffles side to side in a jagged two-step, drunk, strangers weaving around him without looking up from their phones. In the bathroom I wash my face at the sink and, lifting my head, see that I stand between two mirrors. I look hard behind me into each of the untold cascading reflections, as if for variation, or a center, but they only grow smaller and less precise the deeper I look.

The garage where my father worked as a mechanic, two years before I was born, his locker defaced.

He remembers the spray paint ran down to the floor.

That it ran down the center of the locker from the *gg*.

That his boss made him clean it up.

Then: my parents' station wagon, my two short olive arms climbing over the back of the seat and throwing themselves across the arms of my mother. As if to ask a question or convey a truth. My mother smiles at the affection.

*

One plus one equals three.

*

In Switzerland, the German professor of North American Literature says of white supremacist efforts in the antebellum period, trying to contextualize for my classmates:

Think of the Nazis. Is it not the same gesture?

Affirmation of self by subjugation and oppression of other.

It is nothing new.

It has been centuries that we do this to one another.

I cannot raise my hand to say I think it is a violence to equate one atrocity for another.

We've been doing this to one another for centuries, I mumble.

Bewildered, I ask: *So the two of you just never got anywhere with all this—simply agreed to disagree about something this complex, this deep?* He says, *What's complicated! I loved your mother. Her. Not the body. Don't tell me you don't understand that either.*

A blackstart lands on a branch above the man outside; the tree—I don't know what kind it is—is leafless in summer.

*

Omi rubs salt into my skin, then circles a raw egg around my head, chanting to herself. My mother leaves the room: *Witchcraft.* Omi asks: *Fehmti, wildi? Do you understand, my son?*

I respond: *Iyyeh. Yes. What I am asking is do you understand how we bring ourselves here where we are something else. Do we carry the land with us to the new land. Yes, in us the land meets the land.*

*

Who is she to me? My wife, C—
        You know how I mean that, Dad.

Fine. To me, she is Black and an African.
        But if you believe that—I cover then his dessert menu with my hand—*how could you say the things you said all my life, those things you said you know which ones I mean?*

Listen—I've known plenty of white niggers in my day, too.

69

Heidegger says *Man acts as though he were the shaper and master of language, while in fact language remains the master of man.*

My mother says *I am not African American, I am an Arab.*

My friend Solmaz writes *It matters what you call a thing.*

Heidegger says *Language is the house of the truth of Being.*

Majid says *Here they think I am a Dominican. I do not understand.*

Omi says *Hada sweena, hada khiba.*

Therefore: *The master of man is the house of the truth of Being.*

*

~~At what point does~~ the untrue ~~become~~ real

Is it ~~when we give the thing~~ a name   ~~How can~~ we know

Who gets to ~~say~~   ~~Does the thing~~ have one name

For everyone   ~~Everywhere~~ Do you see ~~why~~ it ~~matters~~

I wish ~~it did not matter~~   ~~Who gets to say~~

So do you have a black wife?
    Yes.

Does it matter?
    No. Or, it depends who you ask.

Can the thing matter and not matter at once?
    Not to the same person.

Are you sure?
    The face can be a wound and a shield.

Is the mule both horse and donkey? Neither?
    It depends on the eyes that do the looking.

Can the thing possess both shame and privilege?
    There is no identity.

Why does the construct not bend with our bodies?
    You're losing me.

You remember it's a construct right?
    The mule?

Why do we hold ourselves fixed when we are hurting so?
    Humans crave what is familiar.

How do we honor and free at once?
    To free is to honor, I think.

Can the negro be white, the white man a negro?
    If the room is neither cold nor hot.

Are they the same? Who what here how   is they
    It depends on the looking.

What do we lose?
    Much.

Where is the way out?

I wash the face first,
           A heavy swipe from top
To bottom, not at all gentle,
           Then trace the sponge
Along the length of her nose,
           Water sliding
Down each cheek, then falling
           Over the edge of her
Body—resting, quiet, bare,
           Open to being,
Only now, without condition—
           A net of fish
Cut open from below, freed
           Of its own purpose.
I remove each ring and, speaking,
           To myself, if not to her,
Slide my fingers through the hair
           She had worked
To keep straight, a damp heaviness
           I palm, and begin
To braid each curling tress,
           Tying her
Back to herself—
           Turning her face
I scrub the back of the neck,
           A field of serpents, reaching
Into the braids, an empty
           Wide desert
Where I will place her body
           Into fire, freeing
Her from her containment,
           Releasing. In the room,

I cut the wide linen cloth
          Into thin strips,
Bindings for each limb, and wrap
          The neck, the slow
Division of a body from its mind.
          Quiet now. Quiet.
I circle the table three times,
          Certain not to lift
My hand from the fact of her
          And study her breasts,
Still peaked, her nipples inverted,
          Areolas as two purple songs.
I cover them. I tie the cloth
          Tight around her chest,
And lifting each arm, loop the cloth
          Around the length of each.
Dark tips of fingers extend west and east.
          How does her body speak
Without its breath? I am tired of listening.
          Quickly, I bind each foot,
Each ankle and leg, and keep open
          My eyes as I clean the center of her,
Hairless, honorable, dead—
          The Qur'an calling back to me,
Its splayed pages lifted by a wind
          That has come from nowhere,
The blackness of her body
          Cold inside my hands,
Which know nothing.

"Gnawa Boy, Marrakesh, 1968": The Gnawa are an ethnic group indigenous to West and North Africa.

"Wanting to Be White" is after Jorie Graham. The italicized text is lifted from her poem "Wanting a Child."

"Tippu Tip on His Deathbed in Stone Town": Tippu Tip (1837–1905) was a notoriously violent leader of the Arab slave trade. Tip, the son of Muscat Arab and Swahili traders, was based in Zanzibar and predominantly owned black slaves, though he himself was black.

"'A Mouthful of Salt . . . / I Came through Numb Waters'" is after Morgan Parker. The poem takes its title from her poem "I Know Why the Jive-Ass Bird Sings."

"Passing" is for all the attendees of the 2013 Cave Canem retreat.

"Auction / Roman Girl" is after *A Roman Slave Market* by French painter Jean-Léon Gérôme (1824–1904).

"Preface" is after Franz Wright. The italicized text is lifted from his poem "P.S."

"Landswept": The concept of *landswept* "describes a place or places where everything, both material and immaterial, has been brushed aside, purloined, swept away, blown down, irrigated off, everything except the touchable earth"; it's from "Mural" by Mahmoud Darwish.

"Haratin Girl, Marrakesh, 1968": The Haratin are an ethnic group indigenous to West and North Africa.

"'Your Foot, Your Root'" borrows its title from "Daddy" by Sylvia Plath. The poem is for my father with love. The quoted lines "There is no identity" and "It matters what you call a thing" come, respectively, from Darwish's *In the Presence of Absence* and Solmaz Sharif's *Look*.

"Whiteness on Her Deathbed" is for my mother with love.

Grateful acknowledgement is made to the following publications, where a number of these poems first appeared, sometimes in different versions:

Academy of American Poets , Poem-a-Day Program: "Plantation"
Adroit Journal: "Asmar," "Passing"
Apogee: "Clean Slate"
Baffler: "Song"
Boston Review: "A Mouthful of Salt . . . / I Came through Numb Waters"
Callaloo: "Trying to Live," "Whiteness on Her Deathbed"
Day One: "On This Hard Bench"
Explosion-Proof: "Soho (London)"
Hunger Mountain: "Auction / Roman Girl," "Where If Not Here,"
    "Where If Not Here (II)"
iO: "Tippu Tip on His Deathbed in Stone Town," "Trying to Speak"
Literary Hub: "Wanting to Be White"
Manhattanville Review: "Homosexuality"
New Republic: "Gnawa Boy, Marrakesh, 1968"
Phantom Books: "Into Each Room We Enter without Knowing"
Poetry International: "Haratin Girl, Marrakesh, 1968"
Prairie Schooner: "At *L'Express* French Bistro My White Father Kisses
    My Black Mother Then Calls the Waiter a Nigger," "Eunuch," "The
    Most Opaque Sands Make for the Clearest Glass," "Origin"

My heartfelt thanks to Jon Tribble, the Crab Orchard Series in Poetry editor, and to Allison Joseph, for choosing my book. Thanks, too, to Kwame Dawes and Ashley Strosnider, editors of *Prairie Schooner*, for selecting me as the recipient of the 2015 Edward Stanley Poetry Award, and to Wesley McNair, for awarding me an Academy of American Poets university prize for some of the poems in this collection.

My profound gratitude belongs to the friends who have sustained me and to the teachers and colleagues who have provided essential support of my work. For your generosity of time and spirit, and for your encouragement, offered at times unknowingly or in the smallest ways, thank you: Chris Abani, Maryam Afaq, Elizabeth Alexander, Sarah Arvio, Derrick Austin, Rachel Axelbank,

Adrienne Brock, Mary Kate Burke, Cyrus Cassells, Tina Chang, Jeremy Clark, Henri Cole, Peter Covino, Adam Dalva, DéLana Dameron, Simona di Taranto, Craig Dworkin, Safia Elhillo, Black Excellence, Robin Fein, Francesca Frigo, Hafizah Geter, Jack Gilbert (1925–2012), Aracelis Girmay, Hillary Gulley, Kimiko Hahn, Nathalie Handal, Reginald Harris, Terrance Hayes, Edward Hirsch, Marie Howe, Alan Ince, Julia Ioffe, Raven Jackson, Anne Jamison, Larry Kaplun, Kevin Kavanah, Christo Koutroulis, Boguslaw Krysinski, Brett Fletcher Lauer, Sydney Lea, Rosaria Lecci, Gary Lenhart, Steven Leyva, Chrissy Malvasi, David McLoghlin, Alison Meyers, Dante Micheaux, Candice Morgan, Jerome Murphy, Angel Nafis, Dominique Nagpal, Anh-Thu Ngo, Katharina and Kurt Nuspliger and the Nuspliger family, Elsbeth Pancrazi, Ed Pavlić, Carl Phillips, Therí Pickens, Ben Purkert, Camille Rankine, Matthew Rohrer, Paul Romero, Ronit Rubinstein, Corinne Schneider, Ivy Schweitzer, Nicole Sealey, Ali Shames-Dawson, Naomi Shepherd, Kevin Simmonds, Danez Smith, Patricia Smith, Tracy K. Smith, Barry Tagrin, Johanna Treffy, Natasha Trethewey, Alice Quinn, Lyrae Van Clief–Stefanon, Tom Vogl, Anthe Vorkas, Maya Washington, Afaa Michael Weaver, Maddy Weinfield, Margaret Williamson, L. Lamar Wilson, Jenny Xie, Wendy Xu, Melissa Zeiger, and Rachel Zucker.

Special thanks to Linda Gregg, for showing me the way in; to Timothy Liu and Shara McCallum, for your early attention to the manuscript; to Ama Codjoe, for your sharp eye and diamond-studded antlers, and to Iain Haley Pollock, for your exquisite close reading of the book, both in the final hour; to Morgan Parker, for helping me to believe; to Robin Coste Lewis, for my single grit and lantern; to Daniela Vasquez, for your unfailing sisterhood; and to Niklaus, *immer mein habib*, for our years.

Immeasurable and unspeakable gratitude to the Cave Canem family. To our guides, Toi Derricotte and Cornelius Eady: thank you for giving me the chance to be a brick in the house we are building.

To the New York University creative writing community, especially Deborah Landau and my teachers Catherine Barnett, Yusef Komunyakaa, and Sharon Olds, I owe an enormous debt of gratitude. Likewise, I'm grateful to the Frost Place and the Millay Colony for the Arts, and to my new colleagues and teachers in the Creative Writing Program at Stanford University.

Finally, to my family—Mom, Dad, Anwar, and Karim—I offer this book, humbly, with compassion for what we have inherited and love for what we will continue to build.

Other Books in the Crab Orchard Series in Poetry

Muse
Susan Aizenberg

Millennial Teeth
Dan Albergotti

Hijra
Hala Alyan

Instructions,
Abject & Fuming
Julianna Baggott

Lizzie Borden in Love:
Poems in Women's Voices
Julianna Baggott

This Country of Mothers
Julianna Baggott

The Black Ocean
Brian Barker

The Sphere of Birds
Ciaran Berry

White Summer
Joelle Biele

Gold Bee
Bruce Bond

Rookery
Traci Brimhall

USA-1000
Sass Brown

In Search of the Great Dead
Richard Cecil

Twenty First Century Blues
Richard Cecil

Circle
Victoria Chang

Errata
Lisa Fay Coutley

Salt Moon
Noel Crook

Consolation Miracle
Chad Davidson

From the Fire Hills
Chad Davidson

The Last Predicta
Chad Davidson

Furious Lullaby
Oliver de la Paz

Names above Houses
Oliver de la Paz

The Star-Spangled Banner
Denise Duhamel

Smith Blue
Camille T. Dungy

Seam
Tarfia Faizullah

Beautiful Trouble
Amy Fleury

Sympathetic Magic
Amy Fleury

Soluble Fish
Mary Jo Firth Gillett

Pelican Tracks
Elton Glaser

Winter Amnesties
Elton Glaser

Strange Land
Todd Hearon

Always Danger
David Hernandez